H$_2$O Science

by Jean Stangl

Fearon Teacher Aids
Simon & Schuster
Supplementary
Education Group

Editor: Carol Williams
Illustration: Corbin Hillam
Design: Dianne Platner

ISBN 0-8224-3604-3

Printed in the United States of America
1. 9 8 7 6 5 4 3 2 1

Contents

Introduction

❏ Water is one of the most versatile materials for science discovery. It is also one of the least expensive! Water holds a special fascination for children of all ages, is easy to obtain, presents few clean-up problems, and provides a multitude of learning experiences for young scientists. *H₂O Science* is an easy-to-follow resource book containing experiments using water as the basic material.

❏ A classroom water lab or discovery center can be set up and disassembled within a few minutes. Collect the basic materials—clear plastic drinking glasses, large clear bowls, clean margarine tubs, stirring rods or wooden craft sticks, measuring cups and spoons. Provide a storage space and make paper towels and sponges available for clean-up.

❏ Experiments are set up for small groups of four to six students. Write the materials needed for each activity on a chart and have your young scientists be responsible for gathering materials, cleaning up, and returning materials to the proper places.

❏ Each experiment should be tested before presenting it to the class. Many of the questions in the activities are open-ended, and any logical answer should be accepted. Importance should be placed on the hands-on process of experimentation.

❏ At the beginning of each lesson, define terms, demonstrate concepts that will be used in experimentation, review scientific principles, pose questions, and stimulate student thinking using the discussion material on the teacher's information page. Next, convey the purpose of the experiment to the students and give necessary instructions. Then, allow students to gather materials and follow the lab sheet procedure independently. Students will be required to read and follow directions, estimate, predict, test, measure, observe, and record while making fascinating and valuable discoveries about water. Finally, discuss as a class results the students obtained and what scientific principles were discovered. Clear up any erroneous notions based on inaccurate experimentation, using the information provided in the "Teacher's Notes" section.

❏ Students will enjoy experimenting, and, at the same time, they will learn some methods used by scientists, explore the wonders of water, and discover some of the basic concepts and principles of science. These hands-on activities will stimulate your students' interest in science and will encourage careful investigation, keen observations, logical thinking, and accurate record keeping. With *H₂O Science* you can provide interesting and worthwhile science experiences for your students whether or not you consider science your area of strength.

Chapter 1

The Wonders of Water

H₂O

Purpose: To discover that water exists in three states

Discussion

Materials for Demonstration

electric coffee or teapot, vaporizer, or bottle warmer

sheet of colored construction paper

water

Water is the only material that exists naturally in three states—liquid, solid (ice), and gas (water vapor). Ask students to give examples of each.

Each molecule of water is made up of two atoms of hydrogen and one atom of oxygen. We can't see the molecules, but we can see how they react through observable changes. For example, we see ice form when liquid water freezes. We cannot see the visible water vapor that is always in the air, but we can see that it condenses to form clouds.

Demonstrate water in a gaseous form by heating water in an electric coffee or teapot, vaporizer, or bottle warmer. Hold a sheet of colored construction paper over the steam until the paper is wet. Heat changes liquid water to gas, and the gas spreads above the pot where the warm air rises and cools.

Materials

For each group of 4–6 students:
- clear plastic drinking glass
- bowl
- 10 ice cubes (if not available at school, bring ice from home in a wide-mouth thermos)
- small mirror
- lab sheet for each group member (page 7)

Teacher's Notes

❑ The outside of the glass filled with ice will be covered with drops of water. When the water vapor in the air is chilled, it turns into liquid water.

❑ The water in the bowl can be changed back to a solid by freezing it. Heat changes the solid ice cube into liquid water.

❑ Students will discover in step 8 that our breath contains moisture.

Lab Sheet

H₂O

1. Fill the glass with ice cubes.

2. Set the glass in the bowl.

3. Wait 2 minutes and then feel the outside of the glass. Is it warm or cold?

   _____

4. Wait another 2 minutes and then feel the outside of the glass. Is it wet or dry?

   _____

5. Observe the small drops of water on the outside of the glass. Where did they come from?

   _____

   This shows that when water vapor in the air is chilled, it turns into a _____.

6. Are the ice cubes melting?

   _____

   This shows that heat changes a solid to a _____.

7. How could the liquid water be changed back to its solid form?

   _____

8. Hold the mirror in your hand, open your mouth wide, and exhale onto the mirror. Explain what appears on the mirror.

   _____

   _____

9. The three forms of water are

   _____ , _____ , _____.

H₂O Science © 1990 Fearon Teacher Aids

Amazing Water

Purpose: To discover the meanings of *absorb*, *evaporate*, and *repel*

Materials for Demonstration
paper towel
piece of plastic wrap
water

Discussion

Define and demonstrate each of the following terms.

Absorb—to soak up
Soak the paper towel in the water. The paper towel *absorbs* the water.

Evaporate—to change from a liquid to a gas
Squeeze out the paper towel. Make a spot on the chalkboard with the wet paper towel. The chalkboard absorbs some of the water, but soon the water is drawn up into the air in the form of water vapor. The water *evaporated* from the chalkboard.

Repel—to resist absorbing a liquid
Soak the paper towel in water again. Hold a piece of plastic wrap against the chalkboard and squeeze the wet paper towel against it. The water runs down the piece of plastic wrap. The plastic wrap *repels* water.

Materials

For each group of 4–6 students:
  medicine dropper
  cup
  water
  tub or pail
  sponge
  pinecone
  porous rock or piece of broken
    clay pot
  small piece of wood
  2 paper towels
  lab sheet for each group
    member (pages 10–11)
  6-inch square pieces of:
    construction paper
    waxed paper
    aluminum foil
    newspaper
    fabric
    Styrofoam

Teacher's Notes

❏ Evaporation activities work best on days when the air is dry. If the weather is overcast or humid, it will affect the experiments somewhat but will present opportunities to discuss moisture in the air.

❏ Have students make their predictions in parts A and B before they gather materials for experimentation.

❏ In part C, students will notice that the paper towel in the sun dries faster.

❏ Encourage students to use logical thinking to answer the questions in part D: The sponge will be heavier because it still contains water—not all of it has evaporated. A duck's feathers are coated with oil and the paper is coated with wax—both the oil and wax repel water.

Name _____

Lab Sheet

Amazing Water

A. 1. Put an **A** next to the items you predict will **absorb** water and an **R** next to the items you predict will **repel** water in the "Predictions" column.

2. Fill the cup 1/2 full of water. Fill the medicine dropper with water from the cup and squeeze two drops of water onto each item below.

	Predictions	Test Results
construction paper	_____	_____
waxed paper	_____	_____
aluminum foil	_____	_____
newspaper	_____	_____
fabric	_____	_____
Styrofoam	_____	_____

3. Record your test results by putting an **A** or **R** for each item in the column labeled "Test Results."

B. 1. Circle the items below that you predict will absorb water.

_____ **sponge** _____

_____ **pinecone** _____

_____ **porous rock** _____

_____ **wood** _____

2. Fill the tub or pail with water and place all the items listed in step 1 in the water. Observe for a few minutes. Put an **X** on the lines to the left of the items in step 1 that absorbed water.

H_2O Science © 1990 Fearon Teacher Aids

Amazing Water

3. How did the appearance of each item change? Write your answers on the lines that follow each item in step 1.

C. Wet two paper towels. Squeeze them out and open them up flat. Place one in the sun and one in the shade.

From which paper towel did the water evaporate most quickly? Why?

_____

_____

D. 1. Suppose you weighed a large sponge and then soaked it in water and placed it in the sun to dry. Then you weighed the sponge again and found it was heavier than when you began the experiment. How would you account for this?

_____

_____

2. How are the feathers on a duck's back similar to a piece of waxed paper?

_____

_____

The Water Cycle

Purpose: To develop a better understanding of nature's water cycle

Discussion

Heat from the sun causes water to evaporate from the surface of a body of water in the form of water vapor. The atmosphere is filled with water vapor. When air is cooled to a point at which it can no longer hold all the water vapor it contains, the water vapor condenses into droplets of water that form clouds. As a droplet falls through a cloud, it combines with other droplets to produce precipitation. Precipitation is any moisture that falls from clouds—rain, snow, hail, or sleet. The combination of these processes—evaporation, condensation, and precipitation—makes up the water cycle.

Materials

- large pickle or mustard jar with a screw-on lid (available free from most restaurants)
- small stones to cover bottom of jar
- 1 quart potting soil
- several small plants, such as ivy, Creeping Charlie, Wandering Jew, or root cuttings from house plants (place in water well before the activity so the cuttings can grow roots)
- small jar lid
- water
- lab sheet for each group member (page 15)

Teacher's Notes

❑ Have students set up a terrarium. Write the following directions on a chart or on the chalkboard for students to follow:

1. Cover the bottom of the clean, dry jar with small stones and then add about 4 inches of potting soil.
2. Poke holes in the soil with fingers and place the plants in the holes.
3. Bury the roots of the plants or cuttings.
4. Water the plants until the soil is moist but not wet.
5. Fill the small jar lid with water and place it in among the plants to create a pond.
6. Screw the lid tightly on the jar.
7. Place the jar in a well-lit place but not in the direct sun.

POKE HOLES
FOR PLANTS

WATER

4" OF SOIL

ROCKS

❏ This project could be done in small groups rather than as a class project.

❏ As students observe the terrarium over the next few days and weeks, they will see that water evaporates from the soil, pond, and the plants, condenses on the lid, and falls down into the soil. This cycle then repeats itself. This is basically what happens in the water cycle—evaporation, condensation, and precipitation.

Name _____

Lab Sheet

The Water Cycle

Make a picture illustrating the water cycle you have observed. Label your drawing to show evaporation, condensation, and precipitation taking place.

H₂O Science © 1990 Fearon Teacher Aids

Water That's Alive!

Purpose: To discover that organisms exist in various water sources

Discussion

Ask students to help compile a list of different kinds of water. Discuss the water's origin and uses. For example, water flows to the sea in the form of river water and the runoff of melting snow, rain, and irrigation water. Sea water supports sea life, provides power, and is used for travel by ship. Distilled water is water that has been boiled, turned into vapor, and condensed. This water is relatively pure water because salt and other impurities do not evaporate along with the water. Distilled water is used for drinking, in medicines, and for steam irons.

Explain that scientists make discoveries by carefully observing (over a long period of time), experimenting, and recording data. This lab activity will last for five days, and it is important to keep careful dated recordings of observations.

Materials

- magnifying glasses
- rice
- jars
- labels
- "Water Observation Chart" for each student (page 18)
- water samples, such as:
    - lake water
    - pond or stream water
    - stagnant water
    - rainwater (add a handful of dry grass and let it sit for a few days)
    - swamp water
    - sea water
    - tap water
    - softened water
    - distilled water

Teacher's Notes

- ❏ Have students or adult volunteers collect water for observation. Label the jars with the kind of water they contain. Set the jars of water samples in a sheltered place outside during the day. Do not cover the containers or place them in direct sun.
- ❏ Add five grains of rice to each container of water. The rice will decay and provide food for some kinds of water life. Mold and bacteria may also grow on the rice grains. Bacteria are recognizable by the cloudy appearance of the water near the grains of rice. Minute white specks may also be seen moving through the water (tiny protozoans).

WATER TYPE	DAY 1	DAY 2	DAY 3	DAY 4	DAY 5
LAKE					
STREAM					
POND					
STAGNANT					
RAIN					
SWAMP					
SEA					
TAP					
DISTILLED					

❏ Students should be free to observe and examine the containers of water once or twice a day. Instruct students to write the type of water in each container in a space along the left of the "Water Observation Chart" and write the dates for the next five days in the boxes across the top. Be sure students record their observations each day after examining the water samples. Some of the containers will be full of life that students can examine with the naked eye as well as with a magnifying glass. This experiment shows that water is indeed alive!

❏ For an additional project, have students identify the water life in the containers.

Name _____

Lab Sheet

Water Observation Chart

H$_2$O Science © 1990 Fearon Teacher Aids

Chapter 2

Surface Tension

Does Water Stretch?

Purpose: To explore the concept of surface tension

Discussion

One of the characteristics of water is surface tension. Surface tension is the ability of a substance to stick to itself and pull itself together. Water (and some other liquids) seems to be covered with a thin, plasticlike skin. This property of water is what makes it form drops instead of spreading out into other shapes. Have students press their fingers into the fleshy part of their arms. Ask them if their skin breaks. They will reply that skin stretches but does not break. When insects walk across water, they don't break through the water, either, because the invisible skin of the water stretches and holds the weight of the insects.

Materials

For each group of 4–6 students:
   two 12-inch squares of waxed
      paper
   medicine dropper
   cup of water
   magnifying glass
   sheet of newspaper
   a sliver (about the size of a
      match) cut from a bar of
      soap
   clear plastic drinking glass
   2 paper clips
   table fork
   2 toothpicks
   paper towels
   lab sheet for each group
      member (pages 21–23)

Teacher's Notes

❏ In part A, students will discover that a drop of water has a curved surface and that they cannot make a flat drop. Surface tension holds the drop together, but when soap touches the water, the surface tension is broken.

❏ In part B, students will notice the similarities between a drop of water and the lens of a magnifying glass. Both surfaces are curved and can magnify.

❏ In part C, students will notice that the paper clip dropped in the glass will sink, but the one gently placed in the glass by the fork will float. The molecules at the surface of the water attract each other so strongly that they are able to support the weight of the paper clip. The toothpicks will move together because the surface of the water is a little higher near the rim. By touching the surface with soap, the surface tension is broken and the toothpicks quickly spread apart.

Lab Sheet

Does Water Stretch?

A. 1. Lay a sheet of waxed paper on the table.

2. Fill the medicine dropper with water from the cup.

3. Squeeze several drops onto the waxed paper. What shapes are the drops?

_____

4. Pull the dropper slowly through the drop. Can you separate the drop?

_____

5. Touch the drops with a sliver of soap. Did you break the surface tension?

_____

6. Can you make a flat drop?_____

B. 1. Place the newspaper on a dry table. Lay the other piece of waxed paper over the newspaper.

2. Squeeze a drop of water onto the waxed paper.

3. Examine the drop at eye level. Is the top flat, curved, or sunken?

_____

4. Compare the water drop to the lens on the magnifying glass. Are their surfaces alike or different? How?

_____

_____

5. Look at the newsprint through the magnifying glass. How does the print look?

_____

H₂O Science © 1990 Fearon Teacher Aids

6. Make another drop of water on the waxed paper and look down through the drop at the newsprint. How does the print look?

_____

7. What did you discover about a drop of water?

_____

_____

C. 1. Fill the plastic glass nearly full of water.

2. Drop a paper clip in the glass. What happened to the paper clip?

_____

3. Wait for the water to stop moving. Take another paper clip and lay it on the end of the fork.

4. Gently lower the end of the fork just below the surface of the water. Tip the fork and let the paper clip slide off. What happens to the paper clip? Why?

_____

_____

5. Touch the paper clip with the fork. What happens to the paper clip? Why?

_____

_____

H₂O Science © 1990 Fearon Teacher Aids

6. Wait for the water to stop moving. Take a toothpick in each hand and carefully drop the toothpicks side by side onto the surface of the water about an inch apart. What happens to the toothpicks?

_____

_____

7. Touch the water between the toothpicks with a sliver of soap. What happens to the toothpicks?

_____

Why does soap cause this to happen?

_____

_____

The Great Pepper Chase

Purpose: To discover ways to weaken and strengthen surface tension

Discussion

Review surface tension and the fact that the skinlike surface of water is able to support the weight of a lightweight item, such as a paper clip, a needle, or an insect. Ask students to speculate what might happen to pepper, cinnamon, sugar, and liquid soap when each is added to water. Will they sink, float, dissolve, or mix? Record student predictions so that they can be compared with actual results after experimentation.

Materials

For each group of 4–6 students:
   aluminum pie pan
   liquid dish soap
   medicine dropper
   pepper
   cinnamon
   sugar
   1/4 teaspoon measuring
      spoon
   paper towels
   water
   lab sheet for each group
      member (pages 26–27)

Teacher's Notes

❑ In part A, the pepper will "run" when soap is added to the water. When sugar is sprinkled onto the water, the pepper will "run" back. When the activity is repeated in part B using cinnamon, the reaction will be the same. Any kind of soap added to the water weakens the pulling power. By adding sugar, the skin has a stronger pull.

❑ Older students may be interested to know that water is lipophobic (literally, fat fearing) and hydrophilic (literally, water loving). Soap (which is basically fat) is hydrophobic (water fearing) and lipophilic (fat loving). *Hydro* means "water," *phobic* means "fear of," *lipo* means "fat," and *philic* means "love."

Name _____

The Great Pepper Chase

Lab Sheet

A. 1. Fill the aluminum pan 1/2 full of water.

2. Sprinkle 1/4 teaspoon of pepper on the surface of the water. What happens to the pepper?

   _____

3. Using the medicine dropper, squeeze one drop of liquid soap onto your finger. Place your finger in the water. What happens to the pepper?

   _____

4. Sprinkle 1/4 teaspoon of sugar on the water. Watch carefully. What happens to the sugar?

   _____

   What happens to the pepper?

   _____

B. 1. Wash and clean the pan of all traces of soap and refill it 1/2 full of water.

2. Sprinkle 1/4 teaspoon of cinnamon on the surface of the water. What happens to the cinnamon?

   _____

3. Squeeze one drop of liquid soap onto your finger. Place your finger in the water. What happens to the cinnamon?

   _____

H$_2$O Science © 1990 Fearon Teacher Aids

The Great Pepper Chase

4. Sprinkle 1/4 teaspoon of sugar on the water. Watch carefully. What happens to the sugar?

_____

What happens to the cinnamon?

_____

C. 1. Using the information you gained from the experiments in parts A and B, what weakened the surface tension of the water?

_____

2. What strengthened the surface tension of the water?

_____

Attract and Repel

Purpose: To compare the action of soap and sugar when they are allowed to touch the surface of water

Discussion

Materials for Demonstration
sugar cube
piece of soap
toothpick
magnet

Review surface tension. Display the magnet and remind students that it can attract and repel certain materials. Allow students to test classroom items to see if the magnet attracts or repels the items. Ask students if they think other materials have the ability to attract or repel. Show students the sugar cube, piece of soap, and toothpick and ask them to speculate whether any of these items can attract or repel.

Materials

For each group of 4–6 students:
   2 bowls
   sugar cube
   4 toothpicks
   almond-size piece of soap
   water
   lab sheet for each group
       member (pages 30–31)

Teacher's Notes

❑ In part A, students should notice that the pieces of wood are immediately attracted to the sugar cube. The sugar cube is not magnetic, but it is porous and absorbs water. This creates a small current that pulls the pieces of wood toward it.

❑ In part B, students will see the reverse action. The soap gives off a slightly oily film that spreads outward quickly, weakens the surface tension, and pushes the pieces of wood away. Sugar attracts water and strengthens surface tension. Soap repels water and weakens surface tension.

Name _____

Lab Sheet

Attract and Repel

A. 1. Fill one bowl 1/2 full of water.

 2. Break two toothpicks into small pieces.

 3. Place the toothpick pieces on the surface of the water. What happens to the toothpicks?

 _____

 4. Drop a sugar cube into the center of the water. What happens to the sugar?

 _____

 What happens to the toothpicks?

 _____

 5. Try to explain why you think this happens.

 _____

 _____

B. 1. Fill the other bowl 1/2 full of water.

 2. Break two toothpicks into small pieces.

 3. Place the toothpick pieces on the surface of the water. What happens to the toothpicks?

 _____

 4. Place a piece of soap in the center of the water. What happens to the soap?

 _____

 What happens to the toothpicks?

 _____

H₂O Science © 1990 Fearon Teacher Aids

Attract and Repel

5. Try to explain why you think this happens.

_____

_____

Circle the correct answers according to your experimentation.

1. Sugar attracts/repels water.

2. Soap attracts/repels water.

3. Sugar weakens/strengthens the surface tension of water.

4. Soap weakens/strengthens the surface tension of water.

Water on a String

Purpose: To discover that surface tension can cause water to cling to a string

Discussion

Review surface tension. Ask students if they think water can "walk" along a string without falling off and what happens to a string when it is placed in water. Explain to students that scientists sometimes do experiments many times in order to make even a small discovery and that the experiment they will be trying may have to be done more than once.

Materials

For each group of 4–6 students:
  20- and 36-inch pieces of cotton string
  20-inch piece of yarn
  measuring cup with spout and handle
  clear plastic drinking glass
  dishpan
  water
  lab sheet for each group member (page 33)

Teacher's Notes

❏ This is a good activity to do outdoors or over a sink or wading pool. It may take some practice before students can pour the water down the string. The string must be held taut and the water poured **very** slowly. Some students may find it easier to hold the string and to pour the water themselves.

❏ Surface tension is the reason the water clings to the string. Water will also cling to the longer piece of string and to the yarn.

Water on a String

Lab Sheet

1. Set the plastic glass inside the dishpan.

2. Tie one end of the 20-inch piece of string to the handle of the measuring cup.

3. Fill the cup 1/2 full of water.

4. Wet the string in the cup of water.

5. Stretch the string across the top of the cup and over the spout. Have a partner hold the untied end of the string over the opening of the glass.

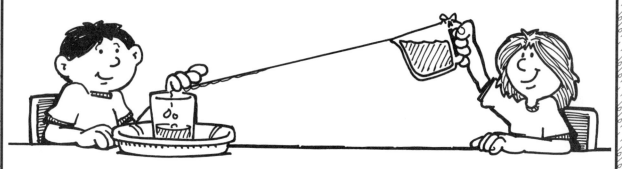

6. Stretch and hold the string tightly.

7. Raise the measuring cup off the table so that the line of the string is at a slight angle.

8. Pour the water out of the measuring cup and down the string very slowly and carefully. Try this several times.

9. Does the water cling to the string? Why?

   _____

10. Try the same experiment with the 36-inch string. Did the water cling to it?

    _____

11. What happens when you use the piece of yarn?

    _____

H₂O Science © 1990 Fearon Teacher Aids

Paper Clip Count

Purpose: To discover how surface tension allows water to expand and make room for small amounts of additional water displaced by a number of small objects

Materials for Demonstration
soft clay
1/4, 1/3, and 1/2 cup nested measuring cups
1 cup liquid measuring cup
jar of water

Discussion

Ask three students to help you with this displacement activity. Give each student one of the nested measuring cups to fill with clay. Ask the student with the 1/4 cup of clay to fill the liquid measuring cup with an equal amount of water (1/4 cup), remove the clay from the cup, and carefully drop the clay in the water in the larger measuring cup. Ask the student to notice the new water level in the cup. Repeat the activity with the other two students. Ask the class to help explain these examples of displacement.

Materials

For each group of 4–6 students:
  clear plastic drinking glass
  measuring cup
  medicine dropper
  paper towels
  piece of cork or Styrofoam about half the size of a small pea
  50 metal paper clips
  water
  lab sheet for each group member (pages 36–37)

Teacher's Notes

❑ For this surface tension/displacement activity, students should work on the floor or sidewalk to avoid jarring the glass of water. Caution students about the importance of pouring carefully so that the water does not overflow. If this happens, they must start the experiment over.

❑ Give each group as many paper clips as available. Between 50 and 100 paper clips can probably be added to the glass. As part of the clean-up, the paper clips should be dried so that they can be used again.

❑ The water should have a convex surface that causes the cork to float to the rim of the glass. If the water's surface isn't convex, there is room for more water.

❑ Surface tension allows water to expand over the rim and make room for the tiny amount of water displaced by the paper clips.

Name _____

Lab Sheet

Paper Clip Count

During this experiment, do not allow the glass to overflow or the paper towel to get wet. Should this happen, start the experiment over.

1. Place a paper towel on the floor. This is your work area.

2. Fill a glass 1/2 full of water. Dry the outside of the glass. Place it in the center of the paper towel.

3. Use the measuring cup to fill the glass with water. Fill it as full as possible without allowing any water to overflow. Be careful!

4. When your group agrees that the glass is full, fill the medicine dropper with water.

5. Carefully add four drops of water, one at a time. Did the glass overflow? _____

6. Estimate the number of drops of water you think can be added before the glass overflows. _____

7. Add the estimated number of drops, one at a time. Did the glass overflow? _____

8. Carefully add four paper clips, one at a time. Did the glass overflow? _____

9. Estimate the number of paper clips you think can be added before the glass overflows. _____

10. Add the estimated number of paper clips, one at a time. Did the glass overflow? _____

H₂O Science © 1990 Fearon Teacher Aids

Paper Clip Count

11. Carefully place the piece of cork on top of the water near the center. What happens to the cork?

_____

_____

(The water should have a convex or curved surface much like the surface of a hand lens. If it does not, the glass has room for more water.)

12. How is this experiment an example of displacement?

_____

_____

13. How is this experiment an example of surface tension?

_____

_____

H₂O Science © 1990 Fearon Teacher Aids

Chapter 3

Buoyancy

Sink or Float?

Purpose: To discover why some items sink and others float

Discussion

Discuss the terms *sink* and *float*. Using student suggestions, make a two-column chart listing common objects that sink or float.

Ask students to speculate what causes some objects to float and others to sink. They may correctly conclude that objects lighter than water usually float and objects that are heavier than water usually sink.

Materials

For each group of 4–6 students:
- **deep bowl**
- **plastic cup that floats**
- **clear plastic drinking glass**
- **100 pennies (2 rolls)**
- **aluminum pie pan**
- **cork**
- **water**
- **lab sheet for each group member (pages 42–43)**
- **plastic dishpan filled with a variety of objects that will sink or float***

Teacher's Notes

❑ Provide each group of students with a dishpan of objects that will sink or float, and have students make their predictions before they fill the dishpan with water.

❑ In part B, as more pennies are added to the cup, the plastic cup will sink deeper. The cup holds air and floats as long as the weight of the cup is equal to the weight of the water that the cup pushes aside. The increased weight of the pennies eventually causes the cup to sink so deep that water is able to enter the cup.

❑ In part C, the pressure, or force, of the air in the bottom of the glass pushes the cork to the bottom of the pan.

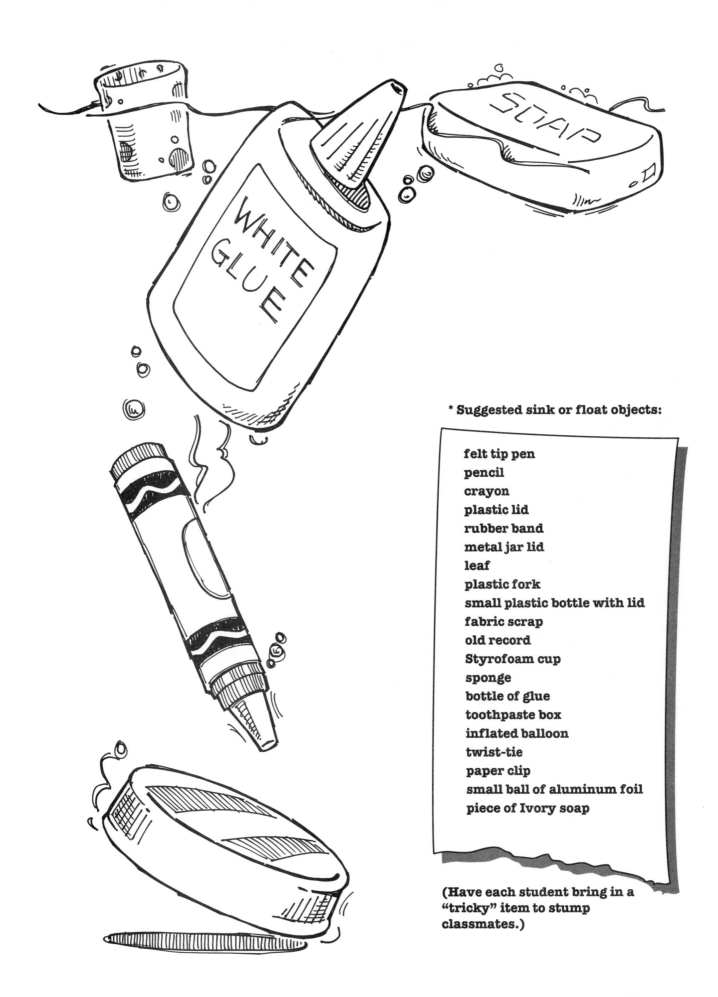

* Suggested sink or float objects:

felt tip pen
pencil
crayon
plastic lid
rubber band
metal jar lid
leaf
plastic fork
small plastic bottle with lid
fabric scrap
old record
Styrofoam cup
sponge
bottle of glue
toothpaste box
inflated balloon
twist-tie
paper clip
small ball of aluminum foil
piece of Ivory soap

(Have each student bring in a "tricky" item to stump classmates.)

Name _____

Lab Sheet

Sink or Float?

A. 1. List each "sink or float" item under the "Object" column below.

2. Predict whether each item will sink or float by marking the "Prediction" column with an S for sink or F for float.

Object	Prediction	Test Result
_____	_____	_____
_____	_____	_____
_____	_____	_____
_____	_____	_____
_____	_____	_____
_____	_____	_____
_____	_____	_____
_____	_____	_____
_____	_____	_____

3. Fill the plastic dishpan with water and test each object by putting it in the dishpan. Record the results with an S or F in the "Test Result" column.

Sink or Float?

B. 1. Remove the objects from the dishpan.

2. Place the plastic cup in the water. Does it sink or float? _____

3. Drop a penny in the water. Does it sink or float? _____

4. Place a penny in the cup. Does the cup sink or float? _____

5. How many pennies do you estimate can be placed in the cup before it sinks?_____

6. Add one penny at a time until water enters the cup. How many pennies did you add before water entered the cup?_____

7. You saw that a penny cannot float in water. How do you explain that a penny can float when it's inside a cup?

   _____

   _____

C. 1. Remove all objects from the dishpan.

2. Drop a cork in the water.

3. Try to sink the cork without touching it.

4. Here's the secret: Hold a glass over the cork and lower the glass until its rim touches the bottom of the pan.

5. How did the glass cause the cork to sink?

   _____

   _____

Salty Water Experiments

Purpose: To discover if salt water has more buoyancy than fresh water

Discussion

Review why some objects float and others sink. Discuss how objects and people float more easily in the ocean than in swimming pools or lakes. Each gallon of sea water contains approximately 1/4 pound of salt. Have students figure how much salt to add to a pint of water to make it as salty as sea water (1/2 ounce).

The volume of salt water equal to the volume of an object weighs more than the object and therefore pushes the object to the surface. Have students predict how heavy an object can be and still remain afloat in a pint of sea water.

Ask students what they think would happen when salt water is allowed to run into a freshwater pond. Will the fresh and salt water mix?

Materials

For each group of 4–6 students:
- 2 wide-mouth pint jars
- egg
- large serving spoon
- 1/2 cup salt
- measuring cup showing ounces
- large mixing bowl
- food coloring
- water
- tape
- felt tip pen
- lab sheet for each group member (pages 46–47)

Teacher's Notes

- ❏ In part A, the egg will sink in fresh water (a very stale egg will float to the surface because it has started to dry out and is therefore lighter). The egg will float in salt water.
- ❏ For part B, have students look around the classroom or outside for items they think will sink in fresh water but float in salt water. Let them test the materials in the two jars to find out.
- ❏ In part C, some wave action should occur after pouring in the salt water. Students will be able to observe the fresh and salt water separate.

Lab Sheet

Salty Water

A. 1. Using tape and a felt tip pen, label one jar "fresh" and the other "salt."

2. Fill the jars 3/4 full of water.

3. Into the jar labeled "salt," measure the amount of salt the class decided was needed to make a pint of water as salty as sea water. Stir well.

4. Place the egg on the spoon and carefully lower it into the fresh water. Remove the spoon. What happens to the egg?

_____

5. Use the spoon to remove the egg. Carefully lower the egg into the salt water. Remove the spoon. What happens to the egg?

_____

6. What does this experiment show?

_____

_____

B. Experiment with some small objects to find some that sink in fresh water but float in salt water. List the objects and tell what happened when you put them in fresh and salt water.

_____

_____

H₂O Science © 1990 Fearon Teacher Aids

Salty Water

C. 1. Add three drops of food coloring to the jar of salt water. Stir to mix the color.

2. Fill the mixing bowl 1/2 full of water.

3. Slightly tip the bowl of water and very slowly pour the salt water down the inside of the bowl near the edge.

4. After pouring all the salt water into the bowl, set the bowl flat.

5. Did the colored salt water mix with the fresh water? Record your observations.

_____

_____

H₂O Science © 1990 Fearon Teacher Aids

Density

Purpose: To determine if liquids have different densities

Discussion

Materials for Demonstration
water
cooking oil
dark corn syrup
1/4 cup measuring cup
3 clear plastic glasses

Measure 1/4 cup each of water, cooking oil, and corn syrup into separate glasses. Tell the students that if one liquid is heavier than another, it is said to be denser than the lighter liquid. Ask a student to arrange the glasses according to density. Then ask students to devise some ways to test the density of the three liquids. They might suggest lifting or weighing the glasses. Suggest that a liquid that is less dense than water will float on water and a liquid that is denser will sink below the water.

Materials

For each group of 4–6 students:
   kitchen scale
   3 identical clear plastic drinking glasses
   1/4 cup measuring cup
   stirring rod or craft stick
   food coloring
   paper towels
   felt tip pens or crayons
   cooking oil
   water
   dark corn syrup
   lab sheet for each group member (pages 49–50)

Teacher's Notes

❑ In part A, students should find that the corn syrup is the heaviest and the oil is the lightest.

❑ In part B, the oil will float on the water because it is less dense than water. Corn syrup sinks to the bottom because it is denser than water.

❑ When an oil spill occurs in the ocean, the oil floats and moves with the ocean current. The oil is carried by the tide to the shore and settles in the sand and on rocks, plants, and animals.

Density

Lab Sheet

A. 1. Measure 1/4 cup of water and pour it into a glass. Dry the measuring cup. Measure 1/4 cup of oil and pour it into a glass. Wash the measuring cup with soap and dry it. Measure 1/4 cup of corn syrup and pour it into a glass.

2. Weigh each glass of liquid and record the weight.

water _____

oil _____

corn syrup _____

3. Which liquid is the heaviest? _____

Which liquid is the lightest? _____

B. 1. Add three drops of food coloring to the glass of water and stir with the stirring rod to mix. Carefully tip the glass containing oil. Pour the water slowly down the inside of the glass of oil. Set the glass flat.

Which liquid is denser? _____

How can you tell? _____

Do the oil and water mix? _____

2. What do you think happens when an oil spill occurs in the ocean?

_____

_____

3. Carefully tip the glass containing oil and water. Pour the syrup slowly down the inside of the glass. Set the glass flat.

Which liquid is densest? _____

H₂O Science © 1990 Fearon Teacher Aids

4. Using felt tip pens or crayons, draw a picture illustrating the three liquids in the glass.

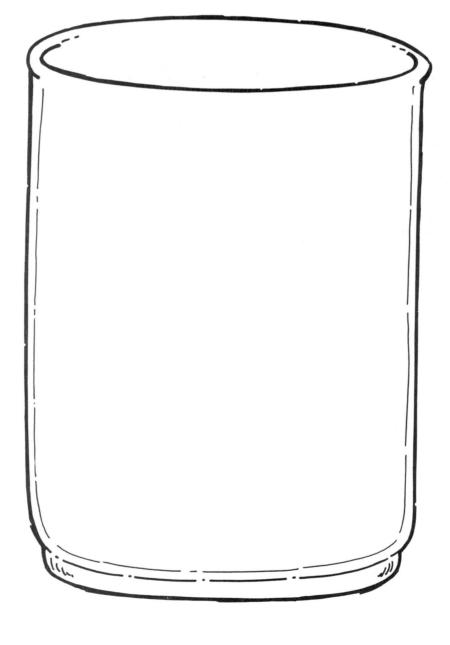

H₂O Science © 1990 Fearon Teacher Aids

Floating Water

Purpose: To determine if the temperature of water will affect its density

Discussion

Ask students what they think happens when snow melts and the cold water runs into warm-water lakes and ponds. Will the cold water mix with the warm water? Do cold and hot water weigh the same or is one denser than the other?

Materials

For each group of 4–6 students:
- plastic mixing bowl
- small aspirin bottle
- food coloring
- hot and cold tap water
- felt tip pens or crayons
- lab sheet for each group member (pages 52–53)

Teacher's Notes

❑ In part A, when students slowly remove their fingers from the bottle, they will observe that the colored hot water floats. Reversing the experiment in part B shows that cold water is heavier (denser) than hot water. As the water temperature evens, the water mixes.

Floating Water

Lab Sheet

A. 1. Fill the bowl with very cold water.

2. Fill the aspirin bottle nearly full with hot water.

3. Add two drops of food coloring to the water in the bottle.

4. Hold your finger over the mouth of the bottle and slowly lower the bottle into the bowl of cold water.

5. Slowly remove your finger from the mouth of the bottle and allow the water to escape. Very slowly remove your hand from the bowl.

6. Draw a picture showing what you observe.

Floating Water

B. 1. Wash the bowl and bottle used in part A.

2. Fill the bowl with hot water.

3. Fill the bottle nearly full with very cold water.

4. Add two drops of food coloring to the water in the bottle.

5. Hold your finger over the mouth of the bottle and slowly lower the bottle into the hot water.

6. Slowly remove your finger from the mouth of the bottle and allow the water to escape. Very slowly remove your hand from the bowl.

7. Draw a picture showing what you observe.

8. Do hot and cold water have the same density? _____

If not, which is denser? _____

H₂O Science © 1990 Fearon Teacher Aids

Chapter 4

Icy Experiments

Cool Predictions

Purpose: To explore water in its frozen state

Discussion

Materials for Demonstration
rock salt
table salt

Ask students for some examples of water in its frozen state (ice cubes, crushed ice, block of ice, icicles, ice on lakes and ponds). Ask students what causes ice to form. (Ice forms when liquid water freezes.) You might tell students that ice is made up of crystals, but the crystals are so close together it is not possible to tell where one ends and another begins.

Display rock salt and table salt. Explain that in some areas of the country, ice forms on streets and bridges in the winter and salt is put on the ice. Ask students why they think this is done, and then explain that salt melts ice because salt lowers the freezing point of water.

Materials

For each group of 4–6 students:
  ice block (frozen in a quart milk carton and then removed from the carton)
  3 tablespoons rock salt
  5 tablespoons table salt
  3 tablespoons sugar
  3 clear plastic drinking glasses
  8 ice cubes*
  1 cup crushed ice*
  food coloring
  stirring rod or craft stick
  measuring spoon
  1 cup of snow (if available)
  water
  lab sheet for each group member (pages 58–59)

Teacher's Notes

❏ Have students do the prediction part of the lab sheet before they gather the materials. After students have completed the experiments and recorded their answers, have them compare the results with their predictions.

❏ For part A, have students do each part of the experiment using different areas of the ice block. The different kinds of salt melt into the ice block in different patterns and at different rates. Food coloring adds interest to the experiment as ice crystals form.

❏ In part B, the ice cube will float in both glasses of water because ice is lighter than water.

❏ In part C, a full glass of ice cubes, crushed ice, or snow would melt to be less than a full glass of water. In fact, it takes nine to ten glasses of snow to equal one glass of water.

*If ice cubes and crushed ice are not available at school, freeze and crush the ice at home and bring it to class in a wide-mouth thermos or ice chest. Or, ask a parent to bring in the ice at a specific time.

Cool Predictions

Lab Sheet

A. Write your prediction to each question below on the lines that begin with a P.

B. Do each experiment.

C. Write your observations on the lines that begin with an O.

A. What happens to a block of ice when you:

1. Pour 3 tablespoons of rock salt on it?

   P _____

   O _____

2. Pour 3 tablespoons of table salt on it?

   P _____

   O _____

3. Pour 3 tablespoons of sugar on it?

   P _____

   O _____

4. Pour ten drops of food coloring on it?

   P _____

   O _____

H_2O Science © 1990 Fearon Teacher Aids

Cool Predictions

B. What happens when an ice cube is placed in:

1. A 1/2 full glass of water?

P _____

O _____

2. A 1/2 full glass of water plus 2 tablespoons of table salt?

P _____

O _____

(Wash and dry the glasses to use them in part C.)

C. If a full glass of each of the following were allowed to melt, would the glass be full of water, less than full, or overflowing?

Ice cubes   P_____   O_____

Crushed ice   P_____   O_____

Snow   P_____   O_____

If snow is not available, explain why you think your prediction is correct.

_____

_____

How Cold Is It?

Purpose: To discover that the temperatures of glasses of ice, ice water, and ice brine vary

Discussion

Materials for Demonstration

thermometers (Fahrenheit and Celsius)

Ask students to tell you the best way to find out how cold something is. Show the Fahrenheit and Celsius thermometers. Explain how the instruments work and how to read them. Demonstrate how each thermometer works by measuring the temperature both indoors and outdoors. Remind students that ice forms when liquid water freezes. On the Fahrenheit scale, 32°F is the freezing point. On the Celsius scale, the freezing point is 0°C. Explain to students that they will be making three solutions, using a combination of water, ice, and salt, and then testing the solutions to see how the temperatures vary.

Materials

For each group of 4–6 students:

Fahrenheit and Celsius thermometers*

3 clear plastic glasses

12 ice cubes

4 tablespoons rock salt (table salt can also be used)

red, green, and blue felt tip pens or crayons

measuring cup

tablespoon measure

paper towels

water

tape

lab sheet for each group member (pages 62–63)

*The thermometers should be unbreakable and/or alcohol, not mercury, and they should be the type used to measure liquid temperatures.

Teacher's Notes

❑ When salt is mixed with ice, it forms a solution with a lower freezing point than water. A mixture of ice, salt, and water makes salt brine, which is colder than ice or ice water.

❑ Students are to use the felt tip pens to show the temperature of each glass by coloring in the column on each thermometer. Be sure to instruct students to begin coloring the column on the thermometer with the color representing the **coldest** glass **first.** Starting at the bottom of the thermometer, students draw a line until they reach the correct temperature, then they use the next coldest color to continue drawing the color column to the temperature of the second glass. They end with the color representing the warmest glass.

Name _____

Lab Sheet

How Cold Is It?

1. Place a piece of tape on each glass.

2. Label the first glass with a red "A," the second glass with a green "B," and the third glass with a blue "C."

3. To glass A, add 4 ice cubes.

4. To glass B, add 4 ice cubes and 1/2 cup of water.

5. To glass C, add 4 ice cubes, 1/2 cup of water, and 4 tablespoons of salt.

6. Wait two minutes. Test the temperature of each glass with your finger. Record the letter of each glass on the blanks below in order from coldest to the least cold.

    _____ , _____ , _____

7. Measure and record the temperature of each glass using the Fahrenheit and Celsius thermometers. Record the temperatures below.

	F°	**C°**
A (red)	_____	_____
B (green)	_____	_____
C (blue)	_____	_____

8. Which glass is the coldest? _____

H₂O Science © 1990 Fearon Teacher Aids

How Cold Is It?

9. Using the matching felt tip pens, make a color column showing the temperature of each glass on both the Fahrenheit and Celsius thermometers below.

Celsius

Fahrenheit

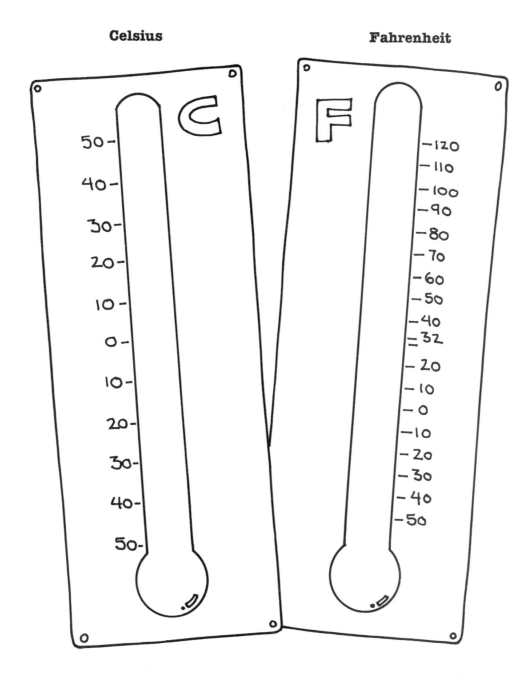

H₂O Science © 1990 Fearon Teacher Aids

Ice Cube Activities

Purpose: To discover some of the characteristics of ice

Discussion

Ask students to share any information they have about ice. Discuss how it looks, feels, and tastes. Discuss what causes it to melt and its behavior in water. Discuss some uses for ice. Ask students to speculate what might happen if a plastic bottle were filled to the top with water, covered with a screw-on lid, placed in a plastic bag, and put in a freezer for several hours. If you have access to a freezer, do this demonstration. If not, give it as an assignment for students to do overnight. Water molecules move about freely, but when water freezes into ice, it expands and the water molecules slow down and move apart. The bottle will break.

Materials

For each group of 4–6 students:
- 2 clear plastic drinking glasses
- 8 ice cubes
- measuring cup
- 1/4 cup salt
- tablespoon
- rubber band
- water
- 8-inch piece of string
- piece of paper
- salt
- stirring rod or craft stick
- blue and red pens or crayons
- lab sheet for each group member (pages 65–66)

Teacher's Notes

❏ Have students make their predictions in part A before gathering materials.

❏ In part B, students will discover that, because ice is dry, the paper will be dry. They will be unable to cover the ice cubes with water because ice is lighter than water and the ice cubes will float. The ice cube in salt water will take longer to melt because salt increases the buoyancy of the ice cube. The part of the ice cube that is above the water will take longer to melt. The water from a melted ice cube will take up only as much room as the ice cube took up when it was floating.

❏ In part C, the salt lowers the melting point enough to melt some of the ice, but the cold ice cube causes water to refreeze around the string. The string is frozen to the ice cube!

Name _____

Ice Cube Activities

Lab Sheet

A. Using a blue pen or crayon, circle the words in the sentences below that answer the questions.

1. Is ice wet or dry?

2. Will an ice cube sink or float in a glass of water?

3. Will an ice cube melt faster in a glass of plain water or salt water?

4. If two ice cubes are placed in a glass of water and allowed to melt, will the water level be higher than, lower than, or the same as when the ice cubes were first added?

B. Discover the correct answers to questions 1–4 by doing the following experiments. Using a red pen or crayon, circle the words in sentences 1–4 that correctly answer the questions. (In some cases, the answer you discover and circle in red may be the same answer you predicted and circled in blue!)

1. Touch a piece of paper to an ice cube. Count to ten and remove the paper. Using a red pen or crayon, circle your answer to question 1.

2. Fill a glass with water. Place an ice cube in another glass. Pour the water over the ice cube. Try to cover the ice cube with water. Circle your answer to question 2.

3. Fill two glasses 1/2 full of water. Add a tablespoon of salt to one glass and stir until mixed. Carefully drop an ice cube in each glass. Observe, then circle your answer to question 3.

4. Place two ice cubes in a glass 1/2 full of water. Place a rubber band around the glass at the water level. Check the water level after the ice cubes melt. Circle your answer to 4.

H₂O Science © 1990 Fearon Teacher Aids

Ice Cube Activities

C. Magic Ice Cube Trick

Can you remove an ice cube from a glass of water without touching it?

Fill a glass 1/2 full of water. Drop an ice cube in the glass. Wet the 8-inch piece of string and place the center of the string on the floating ice cube. Sprinkle a tablespoon of salt over the ice cube and string. Wait two minutes. Take hold of the two ends of the string and presto! You should be able to lift the ice cube out of the water.

Explain why you are able to lift the ice cube with the string.

_____

_____

H_2O Science © 1990 Fearon Teacher Aids

Chapter 5

Siphons

Atmospheric Pressure

Purpose: To discover atmospheric pressure and to learn if water can travel uphill

Discussion

Materials for Demonstration

clean, transparent soft drink bottle

5 clear drinking straws

small ball of clay

tape

water

red food coloring

(Experiments in this chapter should be done in a progressive order because each one builds on the concepts discovered in the previous one.)

Ask students if water can travel uphill, and discuss their comments. Ask students for a definition of atmospheric pressure. Atmosphere is air. Pressure is the force or the weight something exerts. Atmospheric pressure is produced by the weight of the air from the top of the atmosphere as it presses down on the layers of air below it.

Have a student help you with the following demonstration of atmospheric pressure. Fill the soft drink bottle 3/4 full of water, and add four drops of red food coloring. Ask the student to place a straw in the bottle and suck on it to make the water come up into the straw. The student should not drink the colored water. Air presses down on the water in the bottle and helps push the water up the straw. By sucking on the straw, a partial vacuum is created that forces the water up the straw.

Take the clay and push it around the straw at the mouth of the bottle to make an airtight seal. Ask the student to suck on the straw again. This time (if the seal is airtight) the water will not come up into the straw. The clay keeps air from entering the water so there is no air pressure to help force the water up the straw.

Remove the clay and repeat the demonstration. To add interest, tape two straws together (end to end) and have the student suck on the long straw. Add one straw at a time until you have four straws taped together. Either place the bottle on the floor or have the student stand on a sturdy chair or table. This demonstrates that air pressure is strong enough to lift water to a high point.

Materials

For each group of 4–6 students:
  1" x 8" strip of paper towel
  1" x 8" strip of an old terry
    cloth bath towel
  4 clear plastic drinking
    glasses
  straw for each group member
  food coloring
  large bowl
  water
  lab sheet for each group
    member (pages 70–71)

Teacher's Notes

❑ In part A, the paper towel will absorb the water quickly. The bath towel may take up to two hours to absorb the water. Water will travel up through the towels from one glass to the other. Using this process would take a long time to move water from one large container to another, but it shows one way that water travels uphill.

❑ In part B, adding food coloring to the water will make the water more visible. Each member of the group is to place one end of her or his straw in the water, hold a thumb tightly on the other end, and lift the straw out of the water. The water stays in the straw. Because air cannot enter the straw, the water cannot leave it. Atmospheric pressure holds water in the straw. When students remove their thumbs, air enters the straws and the water will run out. Caution students to keep the straws over the water during this experiment.

Lab Sheet

A. 1. Place two glasses side by side.

2. Fill one glass 1/2 full of water.

3. Place one end of the paper towel strip in the water and the other end in the empty glass. What do you predict will happen?

_____

_____

4. Place two more glasses side by side.

5. Fill one glass 1/2 full of water.

6. Place one end of the bath towel strip in the water and the other end in the empty glass. What do you predict will happen?

_____

_____

7. Check the glasses every 30 minutes and record the time and your observations.

H₂O Science © 1990 Fearon Teacher Aids

Atmospheric Pressure

Time	Observations

_____

_____

_____

_____

_____

_____

_____

_____

After careful observation, answer the next two questions.

8. Will water travel uphill? _____

9. Explain how the experiment shows your answer.

   _____

   _____

B. 1. Fill the bowl with water. Add four drops of food coloring and stir with a straw.

2. Place one end of a straw in the water.

3. Hold your thumb tightly over the other end.

4. Lift the straw out of the water. What happens? Why?

   _____

   _____

5. Keep the straw over the bowl. Remove your thumb. What happens? Why?

   _____

   _____

How to Siphon Water

Purpose: To discover how to siphon water

Discussion

Materials for Demonstration
tube
two bowls

(The preceding activity, "Atmospheric Pressure," should be done before this experiment. This is a good activity to do outdoors.)

Ask for student input on what a siphon is and how it works. If students don't know, tell them that a siphon is a simple device that carries liquid from one level to a lower one. It usually consists of a hose or tube that runs between two containers: one filled with liquid and one to which liquid will be transferred.

Set up the procedure for siphoning, using a tube and two bowls but no water. Explain that two bowls must be placed at different levels. During siphoning, the bowl at the highest level and the tube should be filled with water. Explain to students that, when siphoning, they should hold a finger over each end of the tube to keep the water from running out. One end of the tube should be placed deep in the bowl of water and the other in the empty bowl. Both fingers are released at the same time and the water should run up the top of the tube, through the tube, and down into the empty bowl. Tell students that it may take some practice to siphon correctly.

Remind students how water fell out of the straw in the previous experiment ("Atmospheric Pressure") when they removed their thumbs from the straw. As the water falls out of the bottom of the tube, more water fills the empty space and the water continues to flow through the siphon. Air pressure pushing down on the water forces the water up from the full bowl, down through the tube, and into the empty bowl.

Materials

For each group of 4–6 students:
  2 identical bowls
  **24-inch transparent tube
    (1/2 inch in diameter)**
  tape
  felt tip pen
  **large container of water (or
    sink with running water,
    garden hose, and so on)**
  **tables or desks to provide two
    levels of work surface**
  **newspapers or plastic sheet to
    cover work area**
  **lab sheet for each group
    member (pages 75–76)**

Teacher's Notes

❏ Allow students time to practice and experiment
  with the materials before doing the activities on
  the lab sheet. Once the siphon is started, it will
  continue to work until the water in the bowls
  reaches the same level. When both sides of the
  siphon hold the same amount of liquid, the
  liquid will stop moving.

❏ In part B, students will discover that water
  cannot be siphoned to a higher level using this
  siphon method. An outside force would be
  needed to move the water to a higher level.

Name _____

Lab Sheet

How to Siphon Water

A. 1. Place the two bowls at different levels. Use a piece of tape and felt tip pen to label the top bowl "A" and the bottom bowl "B."

2. Fill bowl A 2/3 full of water.

3. Fill the tube with water, then place your fingers tightly over both ends of the tube.

4. Place one end of the tube deep under the water in bowl A and the other end in bowl B.

5. Remove both fingers at the same time. If the siphon does not appear to be working, try again from step 3.

6. Do you think all the water will be siphoned from bowl A?

   _____

7. When the siphoning action stops, observe closely. Draw the water levels of each bowl in the illustration below:

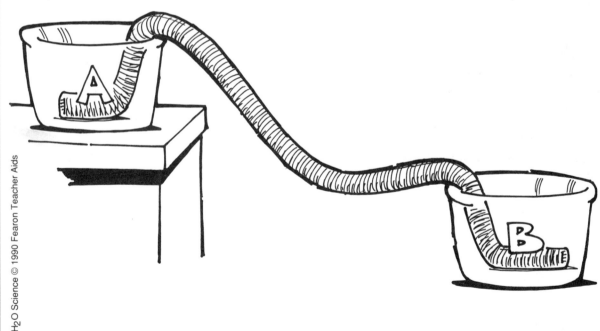

How to Siphon Water

8. Circle the answer that best completes this sentence.

   This experiment shows that a siphon will work

   a. as long as the water in the top bowl stays higher than the water level in the lower bowl.

   b. only until the water in both bowls reaches the same level.

   c. until the top bowl is empty.

B. 1. Fill bowl B 2/3 full of water and empty bowl A.

2. Experiment to see if you can siphon the water from bowl B (the lower bowl) to bowl A (the higher bowl).

3. Were you successful? Why or why not?

   _____

   _____

H₂O Science © 1990 Fearon Teacher Aids

Water Siphoning System

Purpose: To discover how to set up a siphoning system that will produce continuous running water

Discussion

(This experiment should be done after the two previous experiments.) Review the activities in "Atmospheric Pressure" and "How to Siphon Water." Discuss how gravity naturally causes water to flow downhill, how water can be made to go uphill, and how water can be siphoned from one level to another. Display the materials listed below and explain to students that they are to design a water siphoning system of their own using only the materials displayed. They do not have to use all the materials. As a hint, explain to them that the more involved the system, the higher the water source needs to be.

Materials

- several transparent, plastic tubes in different lengths (the diameters should not be greater than 1 inch)
- transparent, clean plastic pipe in different lengths (about 1 1/4 inches in diameter)
- 2-, 3-, and 4-foot-long gutters
- clean trash barrel
- 3 water pails
- assorted containers (dishpans, cans, tubs, bowls, boxes)
- child's wading pool
- lab sheet (page 78)

Teacher's Notes

❏ When students have completed their designs, have them meet in small groups to decide which systems they think will work and which one they would like to try out. Have the groups take turns setting up their best system. After each is set up, discuss as a class whether or not it will work. Take a Polaroid photo before each project is disassembled and the next group begins construction.

❏ When all groups have been given an opportunity to construct their system, post the photos and vote on the most workable system. If possible, move the material outside and let the winning group reconstruct its system and test it. When the project is complete, recycle the water by watering the school lawn, shrubs, or trees.

Name _____

Lab Sheet

Water Siphoning System

Using only the materials displayed in the classroom, design a workable water siphoning system. The system should begin at the barrel and end at the wading pool.

H₂O Science © 1990 Fearon Teacher Aids

Chapter 6

Water Plus

Cabbage Magic

Purpose: To discover one way to identify acids and bases and to discover one way to produce carbon dioxide

Discussion

Discuss how foods that contain acid (citrus fruits, tomatoes, vinegar, and so on) taste. Baking soda (sodium bicarbonate) is a base and can neutralize acids. A base, then, is the opposite of an acid. Explain to students that color can be used as an indicator to show us if something is an acid or a base. The color blue indicates a basic solution and the color pink indicates an acidic solution. Discuss the fact that carbon dioxide is a gas in the breath we exhale and is also in the air and in carbonated beverages. The bubbles tell us the drink is carbonated.

Materials

For each group of 4–6 students:
  red cabbage leaves
  vinegar
  baking soda
  hot water
  medicine dropper
  2 clear plastic drinking
    glasses
  measuring spoons
  spoon
  plastic bowl
  aluminum pie pan
  lab sheet for each group
    member (pages 82–83)

Teacher's Notes

❏ Be sure an adult pours the hot water over the cabbage leaves, and caution students not to touch the glass until it cools.

❏ In part A, when five drops of vinegar are added to one of the glasses, the solution should turn pink. When a teaspoon of baking soda is added, the original color will return. The cabbage leaves contain a pigment that acts as an indicator that turns the water blue. When vinegar (an acid) is added, the color changes to pink, indicating an acidic solution. When baking soda is added, the color indicator reacts again and the solution is basic. The experiments could be repeated using orange or lemon juice rather than vinegar.

❏ When vinegar and baking soda are added to the cabbage water in part B, there is a chemical reaction that resembles a tiny explosion. The acid reacts with the sodium bicarbonate, and one product of this reaction is given off as carbon dioxide. The experiment will continue until the solution becomes saturated and the baking soda will no longer dissolve.

Lab Sheet

Cabbage Magic

A. 1. Tear the cabbage leaves into small bits. Add torn cabbage to both glasses until they are 1/3 full. Ask an adult to add enough hot water to cover the cabbage leaves. Let this mixture sit for a few minutes until it is cool.

2. What happened to the water?

   _____

3. Use a spoon to remove the cabbage leaves and place them in the plastic bowl. (Set one glass aside to use for part B.) Use the medicine dropper to add five drops of vinegar to the solution in one glass. What do you observe?

   _____

4. Add 1 teaspoon of baking soda to the solution and stir. What do you observe?

   _____

5. This experiment shows that:

   Vinegar turns the solution _____

   and is therefore a _____.

   Baking soda turns the solution _____

   and is therefore a _____.

   Is it true or false that an acid is the opposite of a base?

   _____

H₂O Science © 1990 Fearon Teacher Aids

Cabbage Magic

B. 1. Set the glass of cabbage water you saved from part A in an aluminum pie pan.

2. Add 2 tablespoons of vinegar. What do you observe?

   _____

3. Add 2 teaspoons of baking soda. Stir. What do you observe?

   _____

4. Add 2 tablespoons of vinegar and 2 teaspoons of baking soda and stir. Did you get the same reaction as before?

   _____

5. How many times do you think you could continue adding vinegar and baking soda to the solution and get the same results?

   _____

   Draw pictures showing what happened to the cabbage water solution in steps 2 and 3 of part B.

Cabbage Water with Vinegar

Cabbage Water with Baking Soda

Floating Coffee Grounds

Purpose: To discover how gas bubbles can cause coffee grounds to float

Discussion

Materials for Demonstration

bottle of carbonated water or other clear carbonated beverage

clear plastic drinking glass

Ask students what the difference is between fresh orange juice and a carbonated orange drink. How does each look and taste? Have a student pour the bottle of carbonated water into the drinking glass. Discuss any observations. The bubbles will start at the bottom of the glass and rise to the top. Carbonated water contains the gas carbon dioxide, which forms bubbles. Explain to students that carbon dioxide is released when an acid, such as vinegar, and a base, such as baking soda, are added to a glass of water.

Materials

For each group of 4–6 students:

3 clear plastic drinking glasses

wet, used coffee grounds

white paper

vinegar

baking soda

measuring spoons

water

magnifying glass

tape

felt tip pens

lab sheet for each group member (page 85)

Teacher's Notes

❏ There will be little visible reaction in the glasses labeled A and B. In glass C, carbon dioxide gas will form when the vinegar reacts with the baking soda.

❏ When the coffee grounds are added, they will first rise to the top, float, and then sink. They will continue to do this for some time. Tiny gas bubbles form on the coffee grounds and carry them up to float on the surface. When the bubbles break, the coffee grounds sink. If the grounds all float, tap the glass to knock the bubbles off so the grounds will sink. Students can extend the experiment by continuing to add more baking soda and then vinegar to glass C.

Floating Coffee Grounds

Lab Sheet

1. Place five wet coffee grounds on a piece of white paper. Examine them with a magnifying glass. Record your observations.

   _____

2. Using felt tip pens and tape, label the three glasses A, B, and C. Fill each glass 2/3 full of water.

3. Into glass A, measure 1 tablespoon of vinegar and 1/4 teaspoon of wet coffee grounds. Record your observations.

   _____

4. Into glass B, measure 1 tablespoon of baking soda and 1/4 teaspoon of wet coffee grounds. Record your observations.

   _____

5. Into glass C, measure 1 tablespoon of vinegar and 1 tablespoon of baking soda. Record your observations.

   _____

6. When most of the bubbles have stopped, add 1/4 teaspoon of wet coffee grounds. Record your observations and explain the reaction you observe.

   _____

   _____

Bouncing Popcorn

Purpose: To show that carbon dioxide can produce energy

Discussion

Materials for Demonstration

1 cup of water
2 antacid tablets
balloon
transparent soft drink or catsup bottle

Have a student pour a cup of water into the transparent bottle, break two antacid tablets in half, and drop them in the water. As soon as the bubbling starts, have a student slip the balloon over the mouth of the bottle. If you have done "Cabbage Magic" and "Floating Coffee Grounds," the students should be able to explain the reaction taking place. If not, explain how carbon dioxide forms in this reaction. (Antacid tablets contain citric acid and sodium bicarbonate, which react and produce carbon dioxide.) When the carbon dioxide is released, its bouncing molecules exert force against the balloon. As the balloon inflates, students will be surprised to see how much gas is produced.

Materials

For each group of 4–6 students:
   clear plastic drinking glass
   10 popcorn kernels
   2 antacid tablets
   water
   lab sheet for each group member (page 87)

Teacher's Notes

❏ Surprisingly, the popcorn kernels will bounce up and down for several minutes. Most of the kernels will sink to the bottom of the glass when they stop bouncing. Only those that are defective in some way and have absorbed water will remain afloat. This experiment demonstrates that the release of carbon dioxide gives off energy that causes movement.

Name _____

Lab Sheet

Bouncing Popcorn

1. Fill the glass 3/4 full of water.

2. Drop in five popcorn kernels. Record your observations.

   _____

3. Add two antacid tablets. Record your observations.

   _____

4. Wait two minutes and add five more popcorn kernels. When
   the first popcorn kernel starts to move, check the clock and
   record the time.

   _____

5. When the popcorn kernels stop bouncing, do you think they
   will sink or float? _____

6. Record the time when the popcorn kernels stop bouncing.

   _____

7. Watch closely and record your observations of the kernels
   when they stop bouncing. Are they on the bottom of the glass
   or are they floating?

   _____

8. Figure out how long the popcorn kernels were in motion.

   Starting time   _____

   Ending time   _____

   Total time   _____

9. What does this experiment show?

   _____

   _____

   _____

H₂O Science © 1990 Fearon Teacher Aids

Dissolve or Not?

Purpose: To discover if various substances will dissolve in water

Discussion

Ask students what they think *dissolve* means. Have them name some things that might dissolve in water. Ask them to speculate about what happens to a substance if it does not dissolve in water and what might be a possible way to make substances dissolve more quickly and thoroughly (stirring).

Materials

For each group of 4–6 students:
6 clear plastic drinking
   glasses
measuring spoons
6 craft sticks for stirring
spoon
paper towels
aluminum pie pan
1 cup cornstarch
water
tape
permanent marker
lab sheet for each group
   member (pages 90–91)
1 teaspoon each of:
   sugar
   salt
   cocoa
   flour
   cornstarch
   cinnamon

Teacher's Notes

❑ Have students make their predictions before gathering materials.

❑ In part A, students will notice that the sugar dissolves completely. The cocoa and cinnamon will not dissolve, and the salt will not dissolve completely. The flour and cornstarch form a batterlike mixture.

Lab Sheet

Dissolve or Not?

A. If a material dissolves in water, it mixes with the water and becomes difficult to identify or separate from the water. First, predict which of the materials below will dissolve when mixed with water. Write "yes" or "no" in the blank spaces under the column labeled "Predictions."

	Predictions	Test Results
A. sugar	_____	_____
B. cocoa	_____	_____
C. salt	_____	_____
D. cinnamon	_____	_____
E. flour	_____	_____
F. cornstarch	_____	_____

1. Using tape and a permanent marker, label each glass with the name of one of the six substances listed above.

2. Fill each glass 1/2 full of water.

3. Measure 1 teaspoon of each substance into the correctly labeled glass. Wipe the spoon after each use.

4. Place a wooden craft stick in each glass and stir the mixture well.

5. Determine whether each substance dissolved or not and record your results with a "yes" or "no" in the column labeled "Test Results."

H₂O Science © 1990 Fearon Teacher Aids

Dissolve or Not?

B. 1. Pour the contents from the glass containing cornstarch and water into the aluminum pie pan.

2. Add 1/4 cup cornstarch and mix with a spoon.

3. Add 1/4 cup water and stir.

4. Stir in 1 tablespoon of cornstarch at a time until the mixture is like pudding.

5. Pick up a handful and squeeze it through your fingers! (Hold your hand over the pan.)

6. Wash your hands and then write six words that describe how the mixture felt.

_____

_____

_____

H₂O Science © 1990 Fearon Teacher Aids

Diffusion

Purpose: To discover the process of liquid diffusion

Discussion

Materials for Demonstration
glass of milk
chocolate syrup
spoon

Diffusion means to spread out or scatter. It is the intermingling of the constantly moving molecules of liquids and gases. Ask students to describe what happens when chocolate syrup is poured into a glass of milk. Demonstrate, and then stir the mixture. Explain that stirring moves the molecules and causes the chocolate to diffuse into the milk more quickly than it would diffuse if you didn't stir.

Materials

For each group of 4–6 students:
   hot and cold tap water
   food coloring in a squeeze
      bottle
   2 clear plastic drinking
      glasses
   tape
   felt tip pen
   lab sheet for each group
      member (page 93)

Teacher's Notes

❑ In part A, students will observe the food coloring gradually moving in different patterns until all the water is colored. When the color is evenly distributed, it is said to be "in solution" in the water.

❑ In part B, the color will diffuse faster in the glass of hot water because hot molecules move faster than cold molecules do.

Name _____

Lab Sheet

Diffusion

A. 1. Fill a glass 1/2 full of water. Drop in three drops of food coloring.

2. Observe carefully.

3. Explain what you see happening.

_____
_____
_____

B. 1. Rinse out the glass used in part A and use tape and a felt tip pen to label it "cold." Label the other glass "hot."

2. Fill each glass 1/2 full of cold or hot water according to its label.

3. Add three drops of food coloring to each glass of water.

4. In which glass of water did the color diffuse most quickly? Why?

_____
_____
_____

H₂O Science © 1990 Fearon Teacher Aids

Full Jar of Marbles

Purpose: To discover why a container that looks full may not necessarily be full

Discussion

Materials for Demonstration
drinking glass
marbles

Hold up the empty glass. Ask students how they would know when the glass was full if they poured water into it. Stimulate the students to think by telling them that a container that looks full may actually be able to hold more. Hold up a handful of marbles and ask students if the glass would be full if as many marbles as the glass could hold were put into it. Discuss the fact that air occupies space and has weight. Ask students what it means to estimate (to judge, determine, or try to figure out). Explain that in this experiment they will be estimating the amount of material needed to fill a container.

Materials

For each group of 4–6 students:
  clear plastic pill bottle (4–6 ounces with wide mouth and straight sides)
  12 marbles in a margarine tub
  1 cup of table salt
  1/2 cup popcorn kernels
  small funnel
  measuring spoons
  medicine dropper
  glass of water
  lab sheet for each group member (page 95)

Teacher's Notes

❏ This activity is based on Huxley's "barrel of apples" experiment. Thomas Henry Huxley used a barrel, apples, marbles, buckshot, sand, and water to show that even though a container appears to be full, it may not be.

❏ Be sure students estimate the amount of each material needed to fill the bottle before they fill it. The lab sheet tells them to wait for instructions before going on with each step. Distribute one material at a time as it is needed. Also, remind students that they will not be emptying the bottle each time but adding to what is already in it.

❏ Several surprising discoveries (including compacting, absorbing, and dissolving) will be made while cleaning out the bottle, too. Rinse the salt from the popcorn, allow it to dry, and use it again!

Name _____

Lab Sheet

Full Jar of Marbles

1. Estimate and record the amount of material needed to fill the bottle. After completing each part of the experiment, wait for instructions before going on to the next part.

2. Be sure to count the amount of material put in the bottle as you fill it. Do not empty the bottle each time you fill it with a new material. Just keep adding to what is already in the bottle.

3. Record the amount you used to fill the bottle.

    A. Number of marbles estimated _____

       Number of marbles used _____

       Is the bottle full? _____

       Wait for instructions.

    B. Number of popcorn kernels estimated _____

       Number of popcorn kernels used _____

       Is the bottle full? _____

       Wait for instructions.

    C. Number of spoonfuls of salt estimated _____

       Number of spoonfuls of salt used _____

       Is the bottle full? _____

       Wait for instructions.

    D. Number of dropperfuls of water estimated _____

       Number of dropperfuls of water used _____

       Is the bottle full? _____

    E. Compare your estimates with the actual amount used.

       What did you discover by doing this experiment?

       _____

       _____

H₂O Science © 1990 Fearon Teacher Aids